six ingredients

WITH

SIX SISTERS' STUFF

six ingredients

WITH

SIX SISTERS' STUFF

100+ FAST AND EASY FAMILY MEALS

SHADOW
MOUNTAIN

To our husbands—thank you for letting us photograph your
dinner before you could eat it, for still eating our experimental
recipes even when they were bad, and for supporting us and
our crazy ideas all these years. We love you!

All photographs courtesy SixSistersStuff.com.

Any trademarks, service marks, product names, or named features are the property of their respective owners, and they are used herein for reference and comparison purposes only. This book was not prepared, approved, licensed, or endorsed by any of the owners of the trademarks or brand names referred to in this book. There is no express or implied endorsement for any products or services mentioned in this publication.

Visit us at ShadowMountain.com

Library of Congress Cataloging-in-Publication Data
Names: Six Sisters' Stuff, issuing body.
Title: Six ingredients with Six Sisters' Stuff : 100+ fast and easy family meals / Six Sisters' Stuff.
Description: Salt Lake City, Utah : Shadow Mountain, [2019] | Includes index.
Identifiers: LCCN 2019006136 | ISBN 9781629725994 (paperbound)
Subjects: LCSH: Quick and easy cooking. | LCGFT: Cookbooks.
Classification: LCC TX833.5 .S5785 2019 | DDC 641.5/12—dc23
LC record available at https://lccn.loc.gov/2019006136

Printed in China
Four Colour Print Group, Nansha, China

10 9 8 7 6 5 4 3 2 1

contents

SIDE DISHES

DESSERTS

PANTRY STAPLES LIST

Baking Staples

- All-purpose flour
- Baking powder
- Baking soda
- Brown sugar
- Cake mixes (yellow, chocolate, other favorites)
- Chocolate chips
- Cooking spray
- Granulated sugar
- Old-fashioned oats
- Peanut butter
- Powdered sugar
- Sweetened condensed milk
- Vanilla

Spices

- Basil
- Chili powder
- Cinnamon
- Cumin
- Garlic powder
- Garlic salt
- Italian seasoning
- Nutmeg
- Onion powder
- Oregano
- Parsley
- Pepper
- Sage
- Salt

Cooking Staples

- Beef broth
- Bread crumbs
- Canned black beans
- Canned chili
- Canned corn
- Canned mandarin oranges
- Canned pineapple chunks
- Chicken broth
- Cornstarch
- Cream of chicken soup
- Cream of mushroom soup
- Extra virgin olive oil
- Honey
- Noodles
- Onion soup mix
- Pasta sauce
- Ranch dressing packets
- Rice
- Salsa
- Soy sauce
- Taco seasoning packets
- Tomato paste
- Tomato sauce
- Vegetable oil
- Vinegar

main dishes

FALL-APART SLOW COOKER ROAST

Prep time: 10 minutes | Cook time: 8 hours | Total time: 8 hours 10 minutes | Serves: 6 to 8

1 (3-pound) chuck roast

1 (1-ounce) packet ranch dressing mix

1 (1-ounce) packet *au jus* gravy mix

5 pepperoncini peppers, sliced

¼ cup (½ stick) butter, cut into 4 to 6 pieces

½ cup beef broth

Coat slow cooker with nonstick cooking spray. Place pot roast in slow cooker. Top with ranch dressing mix, *au jus* gravy mix, pepperoncini peppers, and butter pieces. Pour beef broth over roast and cook on low 8 hours.

Slice and serve.

If desired, you can prepare an easy gravy to top the roast: melt 2 tablespoons butter in a saucepan over medium heat. Stir in 2 tablespoons all-purpose flour and combine well to make a roux. While whisking, slowly pour in 1½ to 2 cups of the strained liquids from slow cooker. Continue whisking over medium heat until desired consistency is reached. Gravy will begin to thicken after mixture comes to a boil.

Serve with Watermelon Feta Salad (page 146) and Italian Roasted Vegetable Medley (page 129).

BEEF-AND-BROCCOLI TERIYAKI SKILLET

Prep time: 12 minutes | Cook time: 15 minutes | Total time: 27 minutes | Serves: 6

2 cups chopped broccoli

2 tablespoons extra virgin olive oil

3 pounds beef round steak, cut into bite-sized pieces

2 tablespoons honey, divided

½ cup teriyaki sauce

¼ cup low-sodium soy sauce

Set oven to high broil.

Line a baking sheet with foil. Add the chopped broccoli and olive oil to pan and toss until broccoli is coated in oil. Sprinkle with salt. Broil 4 to 5 minutes, flipping broccoli halfway through.

In a large skillet, over medium heat, cook the steak until the meat is no longer red but still a dark pink. Drizzle 1 teaspoon of the honey over the beef and cook until meat reaches desired doneness. Remove from heat.

In a small bowl, combine the teriyaki sauce, soy sauce, and remaining honey until well combined.

Combine the beef and broccoli, and drizzle the teriyaki glaze on top. Serve immediately over hot, cooked rice, if desired.

Serve with Mushroom and Garlic Quinoa Bake (page 138) and Cookies-and-Cream Caramel Pretzel Rods (page 197).

CRISPY STEAK BURRITOS

Prep time: 12 minutes | Cook time: 12 minutes | Total time: 24 minutes | Serves: 4

1 pound strip or skirt steak

1 cup cooked rice

½ cup guacamole

½ cup pico de gallo

½ cup shredded cheddar cheese

4 (8-inch) flour tortillas

Season steak with salt and pepper. Heat a small amount of oil in a large skillet over high heat until oil ripples. Add steak, and cook 3 to 5 minutes per side, depending on how rare or well-done you prefer your steak. For a better sear on the outside of the steak, do not move the steak while cooking; simply flip once halfway through cooking time. Let steak rest a few minutes and then slice into thin strips.

Assemble burritos by evenly distributing steak strips, rice, guacamole, pico de gallo, and cheese over each flour tortilla. Fold up opposite sides, then the bottom, and then roll up entirely to enclose the filling.

Heat a large, nonstick skillet over medium-high heat. Coat the top and bottom of the burritos with nonstick cooking spray. Place burritos in the skillet, seam side down. Cook about 1 minute or until lightly browned and crisp. Turn the burritos over and cook another minute until golden brown.

Serve with Texas Pinto Beans (page 162), tortilla chips, and Pomegranate Salsa (page 157).

EASY HAMBURGER GRAVY

Prep time: 10 minutes | Cook time: 20 minutes | Total time: 30 minutes | Serves: 6

1 pound ground beef

½ cup chopped onion

3 tablespoons flour

1 tablespoon beef bouillon

2 to 3 tablespoons steak sauce

2 cups milk

In a large skillet over medium-high heat, break apart and cook ground beef with the onions until meat is no longer pink and onions are softened, about 8 to 10 minutes. Drain off excess grease.

Stir flour, beef bouillon, and steak sauce into the hamburger and mix well. Slowly pour in the milk and stir to combine. Bring mixture to a low boil, and cook and stir until sauce starts to thicken. Serve warm over mashed potatoes, cooked noodles, or rice.

Serve with Fresh Berry Salad (page 149) and Chocolate-Caramel Brownie Trifle (page 198).

TACO STUFFED PEPPERS

Prep time: 15 minutes | Cook time: 30 minutes | Total time: 45 minutes | Serves: 4

4 red bell peppers

1 pound lean ground beef

½ cup cooked rice

1 (10-ounce) can Ro-Tel Diced Tomatoes and Green Chilies, drained

1 (1- or 1.25-ounce) packet taco seasoning

½ to 1 cup shredded cheddar cheese

Preheat oven to 350 degrees F.

Wash peppers and slice about ½ inch off the tops. Remove all seeds and membranes from the inside. Place peppers in a large pot and fill with water. Bring to a boil, remove from heat, and let sit for 5 minutes. Remove peppers from water and set aside.

In a large skillet over medium-high heat, break apart and brown ground beef until cooked through, about 7 to 9 minutes. Drain off any excess grease. Stir in rice, Ro-Tel, and taco seasoning, and mix well to combine.

Place the peppers in an 8x8-inch baking dish and fill them to the top with meat mixture. Top each pepper with cheese and bake 30 minutes, or until peppers are soft and cheese is melted. Serve immediately.

Serve with Cheesy Pull-Apart Biscuits (page 165) and Muddy Buddies (page 193).

GROUND BEEF ENCHILADA CASSEROLE

Prep time: 10 minutes | Cook time: 30 minutes | Total time: 40 minutes | Serves: 4 to 6

1 pound lean ground beef

1 (15-ounce) can red enchilada sauce

1 cup shredded Mexican cheese blend

8 (6-inch) corn tortillas

1 (15-ounce) can black beans, drained and rinsed

Preheat oven to 350 degrees F. Coat a 9x13-inch baking pan with nonstick cooking spray.

In a large skillet, break up and cook ground beef over medium-high heat until no pink remains, about 7 to 9 minutes.

In a large bowl, toss together cooked ground beef, half of the enchilada sauce, and half of the cheese.

Place 4 of the tortillas on the bottom of the prepared baking dish, ripping them apart if necessary, to cover the bottom of the pan.

Top the tortillas with half of the beef mixture and half of the beans. Drizzle with ¼ cup enchilada sauce. Layer remaining tortillas on top, followed by remaining beef mixture and beans. Drizzle the last of the enchilada sauce on top and sprinkle with remaining shredded cheese.

Cover pan with foil and bake 30 minutes or until casserole is heated through. If desired, top with tomatoes, avocado, and cilantro.

Serve with fresh fruit, Brown-Sugar Fruit Dip (page 154), and Texas Pinto Beans (page 162).

TACO CRESCENT ROLLS

Prep time: 15 minutes | Cook time: 15 minutes | Total time: 30 minutes | Serves: 8

1 pound ground beef

1 (1-ounce) package taco seasoning

¼ cup salsa

1 (8-ounce) can refrigerated crescent rolls

½ cup shredded Mexican cheese blend

Preheat oven to 375 degrees F. In a large skillet over medium-high heat, break apart and brown ground beef until no pink remains, about 7 to 9 minutes. Drain off excess grease. Stir in taco seasoning, salsa, and cheese.

Pull dough apart into triangles and place on ungreased baking sheet. Spoon 3 tablespoons of the ground beef mixture onto each triangle, then roll up into a crescent.

Bake 15 minutes or until golden brown. Garnish with extra Mexican cheese and more salsa, if desired.

Serve with Texas Pinto Beans (page 162) and Apple Carrot Slaw (page 142).

BARBECUE BISCUIT CUPS

Prep time: 15 minutes | Cook time: 12 minutes | Total time: 27 minutes | Serves: 8

1 (7.5-ounce) package refrigerated biscuit dough (8-10 count)

1 pound ground beef

¾ cup barbecue sauce

¼ cup diced onions

2 tablespoons packed brown sugar

1 cup shredded Monterey Jack cheese

Preheat oven to 400 degrees F.

Press biscuits into the cups of an ungreased muffin tin. Mold the biscuit dough to the shape of the cups, going up on the sides; set aside.

In a large skillet over medium-high heat, break apart and brown ground beef with chopped onion, until meat is cooked and onions have softened, about 10 minutes. Drain off excess grease.

In a medium bowl, stir together beef mixture, barbecue sauce, and brown sugar until mixed well.

Spoon this mixture evenly into each biscuit cup. Sprinkle tops with shredded cheese and bake 12 minutes, or until biscuits are golden brown.

Serve with Parmesan Peas (page 125) and Layered Strawberry Jell-O (page 150).

SLOW COOKER RITZ CHICKEN

Prep time: 5 minutes | Cook time: 7 hours | Total time: 7 hours 5 minutes | Serves: 6

1 (10.75-ounce) can cream of chicken soup

2 cups sour cream

1½ cups crushed Ritz crackers

½ cup (1 stick) butter, melted

6 boneless, skinless chicken breasts

Parsley, for garnishing

Combine the soup and sour cream in a bowl and set aside.

In another bowl, mix together the cracker crumbs and melted butter.

Place chicken in slow cooker that has been sprayed lightly with nonstick cooking spray. Spoon the soup mixture over the chicken and sprinkle cracker crumbs on top. Cover and cook on low 6 to 7 hours or high 4 to 5 hours.

Garnish with parsley before serving.

Serve with Italian Roasted Vegetable Medley (page 129) and Easy Homemade Rolls (page 166)

SLOW COOKER SWISS CHICKEN

Prep time: 10 minutes | Cook time: 4 hours | Total time: 4 hours 10 minutes | Serves: 6

6 boneless, skinless chicken breasts

6 slices Swiss cheese

1 (10.75-ounce) can cream of chicken soup

¼ cup milk

1 (6-ounce) package chicken stuffing mix

¼ cup (½ stick) butter, melted

Spray slow cooker with nonstick cooking spray.

Place chicken breasts on the bottom of the slow cooker. Cover chicken with slices of Swiss cheese.

In a small bowl, combine cream of chicken soup and milk and pour over chicken and cheese.

Sprinkle stuffing mix over the chicken and then drizzle butter on top.

Cover and cook on low 4 to 6 hours or high 2 to 3 hours.

Serve with Parmesan Peas (page 125) and Easy Homemade Rolls (page 166).

BACON-WRAPPED CREAM CHEESE CHICKEN

Prep time: 10 minutes | Cook time: 35 minutes | Total time: 45 minutes | Serves: 6

6 thinly sliced boneless, skinless chicken breasts

Salt and pepper, to taste

1 (7.5-ounce) carton chive and onion cream cheese spread

6 slices bacon

Parsley, for garnishing

Preheat oven to 400 degrees F. Coat a broiler-safe, 9x13-inch baking dish with nonstick cooking spray.

If chicken breasts are thicker than ¼ inch, pound with a meat pounder until flat. Season with salt and pepper. Spread 1 tablespoon chive and onion cream cheese spread over each chicken breast.

Roll up each chicken breast and then wrap or roll a piece of bacon around it. Secure with a toothpick, if necessary, and lay seam-side down in prepared pan.

Bake 30 minutes. Adjust oven temperature and broil on high 3 to 5 minutes until bacon becomes crisp. Garnish with fresh parsley and serve.

Serve with Parmesan Orzo (page 158) and Parmesan Lemon Asparagus (page 126).

KID APPROVED

BAKED SALTINE-CRACKER CHICKEN

Prep time: 10 minutes | Cook time: 30 minutes | Total time: 40 minutes | Serves: 4 to 6

½ cup (1 stick) butter

2 sleeves saltine crackers

1 teaspoon Italian seasoning

½ teaspoon garlic powder

Salt and pepper, to taste

4 to 6 boneless, skinless chicken breasts

Preheat oven to 375 degrees F. Coat a 9x13-inch baking pan with nonstick cooking spray.

Melt butter in a shallow bowl and set aside.

Crush crackers in a food processor, or a zipper-top bag with a rolling pin, until they become fine crumbs.

Combine crushed crackers, Italian seasoning, garlic powder, salt, and pepper in a separate mixing bowl.

Dip each chicken breast in melted butter, and then coat completely in crumb mixture and place in prepared pan. Bake 25 to 30 minutes, or until juices run clear and temperature registers 160 degrees F. on an instant-read thermometer.

Serve with Lemon Zoodles (page 141) and Slow Cooker Creamed Corn (page 133).

PINEAPPLE CHICKEN TENDERS

Prep time: 1 hour 10 minutes | Cook time: 30 minutes | Total time: 1 hour 40 minutes | Serves: 6

2 pounds chicken tenders

1 (23.5-ounce) jar pineapple chunks, drained

⅓ cup barbecue sauce

2 tablespoons soy sauce

1 tablespoon honey

2 tablespoons sesame seeds (optional)

Lightly coat a 9x13-inch baking dish with nonstick cooking spray and layer chicken tenders evenly across the bottom of the dish; set aside.

In the jar of a blender or food processor combine the pineapple chunks, barbecue sauce, soy sauce, and honey, and blend until smooth.

Pour ¾ of the blended mixture over the chicken tenders. Cover and marinate in the fridge 1 hour. Preheat oven to 350 degrees F.

Remove chicken from refrigerator and bake 25 to 30 minutes, until the juices run clear. If using, sprinkle sesame seeds over chicken. Serve with remaining sauce for dipping.

Serve with Cranberry-Pecan Sweet Potato Bake (page 137) and No-Bake Coconut Bars (page 175).

SLOW COOKER THAI CHILI CHICKEN WINGS

Prep time: 5 minutes | Cook time: 4 hours 10 minutes | Total time: 4 hours 15 minutes | Serves: 6

3 pounds skinless chicken wings

Salt and pepper, to taste

1 (12-ounce) bottle Thai sweet chili sauce

1 tablespoon sesame seeds

2 tablespoons fresh, chopped cilantro

Set oven to high broil and coat a baking sheet with nonstick cooking spray.

Spread chicken wings out on prepared pan and season with salt and pepper, to taste. Broil chicken for 5 minutes. Remove pan from the oven, flip over each wing, and broil 5 more minutes.

Spray slow cooker with nonstick cooking spray and place wings inside. Pour sauce over wings and toss gently to coat. Cook on low 4 hours.

Garnish with sesame seeds and chopped cilantro before serving.

Serve with Watermelon Feta Salad (page 146) and Caramelized Grilled Pineapple (page 145).

BARBECUE-CHICKEN-STUFFED SWEET POTATOES

Prep time: 15 minutes | Cook time: 1 hour 5 minutes | Total time: 1 hour 20 minutes | Serves: 6

6 sweet potatoes

3 boneless, skinless chicken breasts

2 cups barbecue sauce

1 cup shredded mozzarella cheese

½ red onion, diced

4 tablespoons cilantro, chopped

Adjust an oven rack to the center position and preheat oven to 425 degrees F.

Scrub the outside of each potato and remove any blemishes. Poke several holes in each potato with the tines of a fork and place on a rimmed baking sheet. Bake on center rack 45 minutes, or until a fork easily pierces the skin.

Meanwhile, coat a 9x13-inch baking dish with nonstick cooking spray. Place chicken breasts in prepared pan and cover with barbecue sauce. Bake in oven with the sweet potatoes for the last 15 to 20 minutes of cooking, or until juices run clear and the temperature registers 160 degrees F. on an instant-read thermometer. (If your oven isn't large enough to fit both pans at once, prepare chicken in advance by baking at 375 degrees F. about 30 minutes, or until temperature registers 160 degrees F. on an instant-read thermometer.)

Remove chicken and sweet potatoes from the oven. Shred cooked barbecue chicken with two forks. Slice each sweet potato down the middle and fill with shredded chicken. Top each sweet potato with mozzarella cheese, red onion, and chopped cilantro.

Broil on high 2 to 3 minutes, or until cheese is completely melted. Serve hot.

Serve with fresh fruit, Brown-Sugar Fruit Dip (page 154), and Cake Mix M&M's Cookies (page 183).

BARBECUE CHICKEN TOSTADAS

Prep time: 10 minutes | Cook time: 10 minutes | Total time: 20 minutes | Serves: 4 to 6

8 (6-inch) corn tortillas
1 cup barbecue sauce
2 cups cooked, shredded chicken
1 cup shredded mozzarella cheese
½ cup diced red onion
½ cup diced Roma tomatoes

Preheat oven to 400 degrees F.

Place corn tortillas on a baking sheet. Spread 1 tablespoon barbecue sauce on each tortilla. Top each tostada with 2 tablespoons mozzarella cheese.

Mix remaining barbecue sauce with shredded chicken. On top of each tostada, put ¼ cup barbecue chicken and then sprinkle on 1 tablespoon red onion and 1 tablespoon chopped tomatoes. For extra flavor, you could also top with a pinch or 2 of chopped cilantro.

Bake 6 to 8 minutes. Adjust oven temperature and broil on high 1 to 2 additional minutes.

Serve with Cherry Turnovers (page 205) or Layered Strawberry Jell-O (page 150).

OVEN-BAKED CHICKEN TACOS

Prep time: 15 minutes | Cook time: 10 minutes | Total time: 25 minutes | Serves: 6

12 hard taco shells

2½ cups cooked, shredded chicken

1 cup salsa

1 (1-ounce) packet taco seasoning

1½ cups shredded Mexican blend cheese

1 cup sour cream

Preheat oven to 400 degrees F.

Arrange taco shells in a 9x13-inch casserole dish so they are standing up; set aside.

In a medium bowl, combine shredded chicken, salsa, and taco seasoning until mixed well. Spoon chicken mixture evenly into all of the taco shells and top with Mexican blend cheese.

Bake 10 minutes or until cheese has completely melted. Top each taco with sour cream and any other favorite taco toppings.

Serve with Green Chile Rice (page 161) and Texas Pinto Beans (page 162).

CHICKEN-PARMESAN PASTA CASSEROLE

Prep time: 15 minutes | Cook time: 35 minutes | Total time: 50 minutes | Serves: 6 to 8

1 (16-ounce) package penne pasta

3 to 4 boneless, skinless chicken breasts, cooked and shredded

1 (26-ounce) jar marinara sauce

1½ cups shredded mozzarella cheese, divided

½ cup shredded Parmesan cheese, divided

¼ cup chopped fresh basil, divided

Preheat oven to 375 degrees F. Coat a deep 9x13-inch baking dish with nonstick cooking spray; set dish aside.

Cook pasta to al dente stage, according to package directions. Drain pasta and place in a large bowl. Stir in shredded chicken and marinara sauce, mixing well.

Dump half of the pasta/chicken mixture into the bottom of the prepared pan. Top with half of the mozzarella cheese, half of the Parmesan cheese, and half of the chopped basil. Repeat.

Bake 25 minutes, or until cheese is bubbly and casserole is heated through.

Serve with Cheesy Pull-Apart Biscuits (page 165), a simple green salad, and Samoa Brownies (page 172).

SLOW COOKER CHICKEN ALFREDO

Prep time: 5 minutes | Cook time: 3 hours | Total time: 3 hours 5 minutes | Serves: 4

2 boneless skinless chicken breasts

2 teaspoons Italian seasoning

Salt and pepper, to taste

1 (15-ounce) jar Alfredo sauce

8 ounces bowtie pasta, cooked according to package directions

½ cup shredded Parmesan cheese

Coat a slow cooker with nonstick cooking spray.

Season chicken breasts with Italian seasoning, salt, and pepper and place them in the slow cooker. Pour Alfredo sauce over the top. Cook on high 3 to 4 hours, or until chicken is no longer pink.

Remove chicken from sauce and shred or cut into small pieces. Return shredded chicken to the slow cooker and mix back into the sauce. Stir in cooked noodles and top with Parmesan cheese.

Serve with Parmesan Lemon Asparagus (page 126) and Easy Homemade Rolls (page 166).

AVOCADO CHICKEN BITES

Prep time: 15 minutes | Cook time: 12 minutes | Total time: 27 minutes | Serves: 4

1 avocado, diced

1 cup shredded, cooked chicken

¼ cup shredded Monterey Jack cheese

Garlic salt, to taste

1 (8-ounce) package refrigerated crescent dough

1 egg

Preheat oven to 375 degrees F.

In a medium bowl, mix together avocado, shredded chicken, cheese, and garlic salt. As you mix, the avocado will break down slightly, turning the entire mixture green, but that's what it should look like. You can continue to mix until all the avocado is smooth, or you can leave a few larger pieces of avocado in the mixture. Set aside.

Lightly dust a work surface with flour and roll out crescent dough. Cut dough into 12 small rectangles. (A pizza cutter works great for cutting.)

Place a small spoonful of chicken mixture onto one end of each rectangle. Fold the other side over the top and press the edges together, sealing in the chicken mixture. After stuffing and folding each pastry, place on a baking sheet.

Whisk egg and 1 tablespoon water together and brush over the top of each pastry. Bake 12 to 15 minutes, or until puffed and golden brown. Cool a few minutes before serving.

Serve with Fresh Berry Salad (page 149) and Roasted Balsamic Carrots (page 122).

SAVORY SLOW-COOKER TURKEY BREAST

Prep time: 10 minutes | Cook time: 8 hours | Total time: 8 hours 10 minutes | Serves: 8 to 10

1 (3-pound) turkey breast, thawed according to package directions if frozen

2 cups chicken broth

1 onion, cut into slices

4 teaspoons minced garlic

1 teaspoon dried parsley

1 teaspoon dried basil

Coat slow cooker with nonstick cooking spray and lay turkey breast in the bottom of slow cooker. Pour chicken broth over turkey. Sprinkle on onion slices, garlic, parsley, and basil. Cover and cook on low 8 to 9 hours, or until temperature registers 165 degrees F. on an instant-read thermometer.

Remove turkey from slow cooker, let rest five minutes, and then slice to serve.

If desired, you can make a simple gravy by straining the liquids from slow cooker into a small sauce pan. In a separate bowl, whisk together ¼ cup cornstarch with ¼ water to form a thick roux. Whisk roux into cooking liquids and stir over medium heat 5 to 8 minutes, until gravy comes to a low boil and then reaches desired thickness.

Serve with Cranberry-Pecan Sweet Potato Bake (page 137) or Maple-Roasted Butternut Squash (page 130).

CRANBERRY SLOW-COOKER TURKEY BREAST

Prep time: 10 minutes | Cook time: 8 hours | Total time: 8 hours 10 minutes | Serves: 8 to 10

1 (16-ounce) can whole cranberry sauce

1 (1-ounce) package dry onion soup mix

¼ cup orange juice

¼ cup water

1 (3-pound) turkey breast

In a medium bowl, mix together cranberry sauce, onion soup mix, orange juice, and water until combined well.

Place turkey breast in a slow cooker sprayed with nonstick cooking spray and pour prepared sauce on top. Cover slow cooker and cook on low 6 to 8 hours.

Serve with Cheesy Pull-Apart Biscuits (page 165) and Green Beans with Candied Pecans (page 121).

TURKEY TENDERLOINS AND ASPARAGUS

Prep time: 10 minutes, plus 1 hour marinating time | Cook time: 30 minutes | Total time: 1 hour 40 minutes | Serves: 4

1 pound turkey tenderloins

¼ cup low-sodium soy sauce

2 tablespoons Dijon mustard

1 tablespoon extra virgin olive oil

½ teaspoon dried rosemary, minced

1 bundle asparagus

Place turkey tenderloins in a resealable, gallon-sized plastic bag.

In a small bowl, mix together soy sauce, mustard, olive oil, and rosemary. Pour over turkey in bag, seal, and shake well to coat tenderloins. Marinade in refrigerator at least 1 hour, but 3 to 4 hours for better flavor.

Preheat oven to 350 degrees F. Line a rimmed baking sheet with foil and coat lightly with nonstick cooking spray. Remove tenderloins from marinade and bake on prepared pan 20 to 30 minutes, until the temperature registers 165 degrees F. on an instant-read thermometer inserted in the thickest part of the meat.

About 5 minutes before cooking time ends, lightly toss asparagus with some extra virgin olive oil, salt, and pepper, then place on the baking sheet around the turkey and cook until the turkey is done.

Remove from oven and let turkey sit 5 minutes before slicing and serving.

Serve with Greek Yogurt Fruit Salad (page 153) and Chewy Chex Bars (page 179).

TURKEY TACO LETTUCE WRAPS

Prep time: 10 minutes | Cook time: 15 minutes | Total time: 25 minutes | Serves: 4 to 6

1 pound lean ground turkey

1 onion, diced

1 (15-ounce) can pinto beans, drained and rinsed

1 cup salsa

1 (1-ounce) packet taco seasoning

Boston or butter lettuce leaves

In a large skillet over medium-high heat, break apart and brown ground turkey with onion until turkey is no longer pink, about 7 to 9 minutes.

Drain off excess grease, then stir in beans, salsa, and taco seasoning. Simmer 5 minutes to allow the flavors to meld.

Top each lettuce leaf with a scoop of ground turkey mixture. If desired, garnish with your favorite taco toppings, such as shredded cheese, diced tomatoes, sour cream, green onions, and so on.

Serve with Green Chile Rice (page 161) and Texas Pinto Beans (page 162).

TURKEY CLUB ROLL-UPS

Prep time: 15 minutes | Total time: 15 minutes | Serves: 6

4 large flour tortillas

16 slices deli turkey

12 deli-sized slices sharp cheddar cheese

8 strips cooked bacon

Ranch yogurt dressing (for dipping)

Lay tortillas on a big platter. Top each tortilla with 4 slices deli turkey and 3 slices cheese. Lay 2 strips bacon on top of the cheese and then roll up each tortilla. Slice and serve with ranch yogurt dressing for dipping.

Serve with Texas Pinto Beans (page 162) and Snickers Cheeseball (page 194).

GROUND TURKEY AND BLACK BEAN ENCHILADAS

Prep time: 20 minutes | Cook time: 5 minutes | Total time: 25 minutes | Serves: 6 to 8

1 pound ground turkey

1 (16-ounce) can black beans, drained and rinsed

1 (1-ounce) packet taco seasoning mix

8 flour tortillas

2 cups red enchilada sauce

2 cups shredded Mexican blend cheese

Set oven to high broil. Coat a broiler-safe, 9x13-inch baking dish with nonstick cooking spray. (A rimmed baking sheet will also work.)

In a large, nonstick skillet over medium-high heat, break apart and cook the ground turkey until no more pink remains, about 7 to 9 minutes. Drain off any excess grease. Stir in black beans and cook until heated through, about 2 minutes. Add the taco seasoning and mix until well combined.

Place about ½ cup of the mixture down the center of each tortilla. Roll up tortillas and place in prepared pan. Pour enchilada sauce evenly over the enchiladas and sprinkle the cheese on top.

Broil 3 to 4 minutes, or until the cheese is melted and the tortillas begin to brown at the edges.

Serve with Lemon Zoodles (page 141) and Golden Grahams S'mores Bars (page 176).

ONE-PAN EGG AND TURKEY SKILLET

Prep time: 5 minutes | Cook time: 20 minutes | Total time: 25 minutes | Serves: 6

1 pound lean ground turkey

1 cup salsa

6 eggs

Salt and pepper, to taste

In a large, nonstick skillet over medium-high heat, break apart and brown ground turkey until cooked through, about 7 to 9 minutes.

Add salsa, mix well, and let cook another 2 to 3 minutes, until salsa is hot and bubbling.

Crack eggs evenly over turkey-salsa mixture. Cover the skillet and cook 7 to 9 minutes, depending on how soft or firm you like your eggs.

Serve with Fresh Berry Salad (page 149) and Slow Cooker Creamed Corn (page 133).

CREAMY TURKEY-ZUCCHINI CASSEROLE

Prep time: 10 minutes | Cook time: 45 minutes | Total time: 55 minutes | Serves: 8

1 (6-ounce) package stuffing mix

½ cup (1 stick) butter, melted

4 cups diced zucchini

3 cups cooked and cubed turkey breast

1 (10.75-ounce) can cream of chicken soup

½ cup sour cream

Preheat oven to 350 degrees F. Coat a 9x13-inch baking dish with nonstick cooking spray.

In a large bowl, combine the stuffing mix and melted butter, removing ½ cup of the mixture to reserve for the topping. Add the zucchini, turkey, soup, and sour cream to the remaining stuffing and mix well.

Place the zucchini-turkey mix in prepared pan and spread out evenly. Sprinkle reserved stuffing mixture on top and bake, uncovered, 40 to 50 minutes, or until golden brown.

Serve with Easy Homemade Rolls (page 166) and a simple green salad.

TURKEY TACO MEATBALLS

Prep time: 10 minutes | Cook time: 25 minutes | Total time: 35 minutes | Serves: 6

1½ pounds ground turkey

1 (1-ounce) packet taco seasoning

½ teaspoon salt

½ cup Italian bread crumbs

1 egg

2 teaspoons Worcestershire sauce

Preheat oven to 375 degrees F.

In a large bowl, combine the turkey, taco seasoning, salt, bread crumbs, egg, and Worcestershire sauce until well combined.

Form the mixture into 1-inch balls and place on a rimmed baking sheet. Bake 25 minutes. These taste great on their own or served over Spanish rice and garnished with your favorite taco toppings, such as cheese, sour cream, diced avocado, and so on.

Serve with Slow Cooker Creamed Corn (page 133) and Green Chile Rice (page 161).

BARBECUE TURKEY BURGERS

Prep time: 10 minutes | Cook time: 15 minutes | Total time: 25 minutes | Serves: 4

¼ cup chopped onion

¼ cup barbecue sauce, divided

2 tablespoons dry breadcrumbs

2 teaspoons prepared mustard

¾ teaspoon chili powder

1 pound ground turkey

Heat grill to medium-high heat.

In a large mixing bowl, combine onion, 2 tablespoons barbecue sauce, breadcrumbs, mustard, chili powder, ground turkey, and salt and pepper to taste. Mix until all ingredients are evenly distributed.

Divide turkey mixture into 4 equal portions and shape into patties.

Place patties on heated grill. Cook 5 to 7 minutes on each side, until temperature registers 165 degrees F. on an instant-read thermometer.

Serve patties on toasted hamburger buns with lettuce, tomato, and remaining barbecue sauce.

Serve with Lemon Zoodles (page 141) and No-Bake Coconut Bars (page 175).

TURKEY SAUSAGE SLIDERS

Prep time: 10 minutes | Cook time: 15 minutes | Total time: 25 minutes | Serves: 8

1 can refrigerator biscuits

1 (1-pound) package Jennie-O Turkey Breakfast Sausage, cut into 8 slices

5 eggs

Salt and pepper, to taste

4 slices cheddar cheese, each cut in half

Prepare biscuits according to package directions.

While biscuits bake, cook turkey sausage slices in a nonstick skillet over medium-high heat, turning occasionally, until done, about 15 minutes. Temperature should register 165 degrees F. on an instant-read thermometer.

In a bowl, whisk together eggs, season with salt and pepper, and then scramble in a nonstick skillet over medium heat.

To assemble sandwiches, cut biscuits in half and fill each with a slice of turkey sausage, a spoonful of scrambled eggs, and half a slice of cheese.

Serve immediately.

Serve with Caramelized Grilled Pineapple (page 145) and Italian Roasted Vegetable Medley (page 129).

5-INGREDIENT TURKEY MEATLOAF

Prep time: 5 minutes | Cook time: 1 hour | Total time: 1 hour 5 minutes | Serves: 6

1 box Stove Top Stuffing Mix for Turkey

1 cup hot water

1½ pounds lean ground turkey, lean ground beef, or a mixture of both

1 (2-ounce) package Lipton Onion Soup Mix

2 eggs, beaten

Preheat oven to 350 degrees F. Grease a 9x9-inch glass pan.

Pour stuffing mix into a large bowl and cover with the hot water. Let rest 2 minutes. Add ground turkey, onion soup mix, and beaten eggs. Using your hands or a wooden spoon, mix well to evenly distribute all ingredients.

Spread meat mixture into prepared pan and pat it down flat.

Bake 60 to 65 minutes, or until temperature registers 160 degrees F. on an instant-read thermometer. Let rest 5 minutes before serving.

Serve with Italian Roasted Vegetable Medley (page 129) and Easy Homemade Rolls (page 166).

MAPLE-PECAN PORK TENDERLOIN

Prep time: 20 minutes | Cook time: 1 hour | Total time: 1 hour 20 minutes | Serves: 8

1 (3-pound) pork tenderloin

Salt and pepper, to taste

1 cup brown packed sugar

⅓ cup maple syrup

¼ cup Dijon mustard

¾ cup chopped pecans

Preheat oven to 400 degrees F. Line a cookie sheet with foil and coat with nonstick cooking spray. Place pork tenderloin on foil and season with salt and pepper on both sides of meat. Set aside.

In a medium bowl, stir together the brown sugar, maple syrup, mustard, and pecans. Mix until well combined. Spoon the maple syrup and pecan mixture over the top of the pork tenderloin.

Cook, uncovered, for about an hour, until a thermometer inserted in the thickest part of the meat registers 145 degrees F. If the glaze starts to burn during cooking time, place tented foil loosely over the pork.

Let meat rest 5 to 10 minutes before slicing and serving.

Serve with Cheesy Pull-Apart Biscuits (page 165) and Cookies-and-Cream Caramel Pretzel Rods (page 197).

SMOKY SLOW-COOKER PULLED PORK

Prep time: 10 minutes | Cook time: 8 hours | Total time: 8 hours 10 minutes | Serves: 12

3 tablespoons paprika

1 teaspoon garlic powder

1 teaspoon dry mustard

⅓ cup liquid smoke

1 (3- to 4-pound) pork shoulder or butt roast

1 (18-ounce) bottle barbecue sauce

Coat the inside of slow cooker with nonstick cooking spray.

In a small bowl, stir together paprika, a generous amount of salt and ground black pepper (up to 4 teaspoons each), garlic powder, mustard, and liquid smoke.

Rub mixture all over the roast, covering all sides, and place roast in slow cooker. Place lid on slow cooker and bake on low 8 to 10 hours or high 5 to 6 hours.

Remove meat to a large bowl and shred with two forks. Stir in bottle of barbecue sauce. Pork can be served on buns or bread for sandwiches, wrapped in a tortilla, or atop rice.

Serve with Apple Carrot Slaw (page 142) and Green Beans with Candied Pecans (page 121).

CITRUS AND ONION PULLED PORK SLIDERS

Prep time: 5 minutes | Cook time: 8 hours | Total time: 8 hours 5 minutes | Serves: 12

1 (2-pound) pork butt or shoulder

1 bottle Stubb's Citrus and Onion Marinade

12 slider style sandwich rolls

Coat slow cooker with nonstick cooking spray and place roast in insert. Pour Stubb's marinade over top and cook on low 8 hours or high 5 to 6 hours. Move roast to a large bowl and shred with two forks when ready to serve. Serve on slider rolls.

Serve with Green Beans with Candied Pecans (page 121), tortilla chips, and Pomegranate Salsa (page 157).

SLOW COOKER ROOT-BEER-GLAZED RIBS

Prep time: 15 minutes | Cook time: 8 hours | Total time: 8 hours 15 minutes | Serves: 6

1 (3-pound) rack of ribs

¼ cup spicy brown mustard

1 teaspoon seasoning salt

½ teaspoon black pepper

3 cups root beer (divided)

1 cup barbecue sauce

Coat a slow cooker with nonstick cooking spray.

Baste ribs with spicy brown mustard, then sprinkle with seasoning salt and pepper.

Pour 2 cups of root beer into the bottom of the slow cooker.

Cut the slab of ribs into serving-sized sections of 2 to 3 ribs, then place in the slow cooker. Cook on high 7 to 8 hours or low 10 to 12 hours.

About 15 minutes before removing the ribs from the slow cooker, mix together remaining 1 cup root beer and barbecue sauce in a small saucepan over medium heat until boiling. Reduce heat and simmer until sauce thickens, about 15 minutes.

While sauce simmers, set the oven to low broil and line a rimmed baking sheet with foil.

Using tongs, gently remove ribs from the slow cooker. Place the ribs on prepared baking sheet and brush with barbecue sauce mixture. Broil 3 to 4 minutes on each side, basting when flipping. Reserve the remaining barbecue sauce mixture for dipping. Serve immediately and enjoy.

Serve with Apple Carrot Slaw (page 142) and One-Pan Triple-Berry Cobbler (page 201).

GRILLED PORK LOIN MEDALLIONS

Prep time: 10 minutes, plus 30 minutes to 6 hours marinating time | Cook time: 10 minutes | Total time: 20 minutes, plus marinating time | Serves: 8

½ cup packed brown sugar

½ cup Italian salad dressing

¼ cup unsweetened pineapple juice

3 tablespoons soy sauce

2 (1-pound) pork tenderloins, cut into ¾-inch slices

In a medium bowl, mix together the brown sugar, salad dressing, pineapple juice, and soy sauce. Move half of the marinade to an airtight container and store in the refrigerator for later use. Pour remaining half of the marinade into a resealable, gallon-sized bag. Place the tenderloin slices in the bag with the marinade, seal the bag, and marinate in the refrigerator at least 30 minutes or up to 6 hours.

When ready, preheat grill to medium. Cook tenderloins 4 to 5 minutes per side on hot grill until the internal temperature registers 160 degrees F. on an instant-read thermometer, basting the entire time with the reserved marinade.

Serve with Mushroom and Garlic Quinoa Bake (page 138) and Samoa Brownies (page 172).

GRILLED MEDITERRANEAN PORK KABOBS

Prep time: 20 minutes, plus 4 to 10 hours marinating time | Cook time: 8 minutes | Total time: 28 minutes, plus 4 to 10 hours marinating time | Serves: 6

½ **cup red wine vinegar**

½ **cup extra virgin olive oil**

1 large sweet onion, finely chopped

3 tablespoons minced garlic

2 tablespoons finely chopped fresh parsley

2 pounds pork tenderloin, cut into 1-inch cubes

In a small bowl, make a marinade by mixing together red wine vinegar, olive oil, onions, garlic, and parsley. Place pork cubes in a resealable gallon-sized plastic bag. Pour marinade over top, seal bag, and refrigerate at least 4 hours. For maximum flavor, marinate 8 to 10 hours.

If using wooden skewers, let skewers soak in water 30 minutes before assembling. Remove pork from marinade and thread onto skewers, packing tightly. Generously season pork with salt and pepper.

Preheat grill to high heat.

Grill pork 3 to 4 minutes on each side, until its temperature registers 145 degrees F. on an instant-read thermometer.

Serve with Watermelon Feta Salad (page 146) and Parmesan Orzo (page 158).

BROWN-SUGAR-GLAZED PORK CHOPS

Prep time: 15 minutes | Cook time: 25 minutes | Total time: 40 minutes | Serves: 8

¾ cup packed brown sugar

1 (0.7-ounce) packet Italian dressing mix

½ teaspoon garlic salt

½ teaspoon ground black pepper

8 boneless pork chops

½ cup extra virgin olive oil

Preheat oven to 425 degrees F. and line a rimmed baking sheet with foil.

In a small bowl, mix together brown sugar, Italian dressing mix, garlic salt, and pepper until combined well. Baste each pork chop generously with olive oil and dip each chop in the brown-sugar mixture. Place chops on lined baking sheet.

Top pork chops with remaining brown sugar mixture and bake 20 to 25 minutes.

Once the chops are finished baking, turn broiler to high and broil 1 to 2 minutes to allow the brown sugar to caramelize.

Serve with Italian Roasted Vegetable Medley (page 129) and Easy Homemade Rolls (page 166).

SHEET-PAN PORK CHOPS AND POTATOES

Prep time: 10 minutes | Cook time: 40 minutes | Total time: 50 minutes | Serves: 6

½ cup shredded Parmesan cheese

1 teaspoon Italian seasoning

¾ cup Italian bread crumbs

½ cup (1 stick) butter

6 boneless pork chops

4 cups fingerling potatoes

Preheat oven to 400 degrees F. Cover a sheet pan with foil and coat with nonstick cooking spray.

In a medium bowl, combine Parmesan cheese, Italian seasoning, and bread crumbs.

Melt butter in a separate, shallow bowl.

Dip each pork chop in butter, then coat in crumb mixture and place on prepared baking sheet.

Cut potatoes in half and toss with a small amount of extra virgin olive oil. Place potatoes on pan around pork chops. Season pork chops and potatoes with salt and pepper, to taste. Bake 35 to 40 minutes or until pork chops are cooked through (temperature should register 145 to 150 degrees F. on an instant-read thermometer) and potatoes are slightly browned.

Serve with No-Bake Coconut Bars (page 175) or Samoa Brownies (page 172).

CREAMY MUSTARD PORK CHOPS

Prep time: 15 minutes | Cook time: 15 minutes | Total time: 30 minutes | Serves: 4

4 (6-ounce) pork chops, cut ½-inch thick

1 (10.5-ounce) can condensed beef broth

6 ounces cream cheese

2 tablespoons Dijon mustard

2 tablespoons butter

Freshly chopped parsley, for garnishing

Preheat oven to 200 degrees F.

Heat a small amount of extra virgin olive oil in a large skillet over medium-high heat until oil begins to ripple. Add pork chops to pan and brown 2 to 3 minutes on each side. Season with salt and pepper, to taste.

When chops are nicely browned, pour in beef broth and ½ cup water. Bring liquids to a boil, reduce heat to a simmer, then cover and cook 8 to 10 minutes, or until temperature registers 160 degrees F. on an instant-read thermometer inserted in the thickest part of a chop. Transfer pork chops to a baking sheet and place in the oven to keep warm.

To the remaining liquid in the skillet, stir in cream cheese, mustard, and butter. Cook and stir over medium heat until thick and bubbly.

Remove chops from oven and transfer to a large plate or serving platter. Pour pan gravy over top and sprinkle with fresh parsley.

Serve with Watermelon Feta Salad (page 146) or Apple Carrot Slaw (page 142).

ONE-PAN SAUSAGE AND TORTELLINI

Prep time: 10 minutes | Cook time: 10 minutes | Total time: 20 minutes | Serves: 8

1 pound ground mild Italian sausage

3 cups marinara sauce

1 teaspoon Italian seasoning

1 (20-ounce) package fresh cheese tortellini

1 cup shredded mozzarella cheese

½ cup shredded Parmesan cheese

In a large skillet over medium-high heat, break apart and cook sausage until no pink remains, about 7 to 9 minutes. Drain any excess grease.

Stir in marinara sauce, ¾ cup water, Italian seasoning, and tortellini. Bring mixture to a boil. Reduce heat to low, cover, and simmer 8 minutes, or until tortellini is tender.

Remove from heat and stir in mozzarella and Parmesan cheeses until melted. Serve immediately.

Serve with Cheesy Pull-Apart Biscuits (page 165) and Cake Batter Cheesecake (page 184).

CROISSANT BREAKFAST SANDWICH

Prep time: 15 minutes | Cook time: 2 minutes | Total time: 17 minutes | Serves: 4

4 croissants

¼ cup (½ stick) butter, cut into 4 pieces

8 eggs

12 strips bacon, cooked crisp

1 avocado, sliced thin

4 slices cheddar cheese

Preheat oven to broil.

Slice croissants in half and place on a rimmed baking sheet, sliced sides up.

Cook eggs over easy, 2 at a time. To cook eggs over easy, heat a nonstick skillet over low heat. Add 1 piece of the butter to the pan and let butter melt until it begins to foam. Crack 2 eggs into a small bowl or ramekin. When butter stops foaming, quickly pour eggs into pan all at once. Lift the handle of the skillet and tilt the pan so eggs pool to one side. Hold in this position about 10 seconds, until egg whites don't spread.

Lower handle and let eggs cook about 1 minute, until whites are opaque. Gently flip the eggs with a thin silicone spatula. Season with a pinch of salt and pepper and let eggs cook another minute before gently flipping back to their original position. Cook another 10 seconds or so and then slide eggs onto the bottom half of one of the cut croissants. Repeat 3 times.

Top each set of over easy eggs with 3 strips bacon, ¼ of the avocado slices, and one slice of cheddar cheese.

Broil the open-faced sandwiches 1 to 2 minutes until cheese is melted and the bare, top halves of each croissant have crisped slightly.

Remove from the oven, place a top half of each croissant on a bottom half and serve warm.

Serve with Greek Yogurt Fruit Salad (page 153) and Italian Roasted Vegetable Medley (page 129).

PESTO SALMON

Prep time: 10 minutes | Cook time: 20 minutes | Total time: 30 minutes | Serves: 4

4 (4-ounce) salmon fillets

½ cup packed fresh basil

1 clove garlic

¼ cup grated Parmesan cheese

2 tablespoons pine nuts

¼ cup panko bread crumbs

Preheat oven to 400 degrees F. Line a rimmed baking sheet with foil or parchment paper.

In a food processor or blender, mix together basil, garlic, Parmesan, and pine nuts in ¼ cup olive oil until a thin, smooth paste forms.

Place salmon on prepared baking sheet. Spread 2 tablespoons pesto on each fillet, then sprinkle bread crumbs on top.

Bake 20 to 22 minutes or until fish flakes easily with a fork and bread crumbs are lightly browned.

Serve with Parmesan Orzo (page 158) and Lemon Zoodles (page 141).

LEMON AND DILL SALMON

Prep time: 10 minutes | Cook time: 25 minutes | Total time: 35 minutes | Serves: 4

1 (1½- to 2-pound) salmon fillet

Salt and pepper, to taste

¼ cup (½ stick) butter, melted

3 lemons

2 cloves garlic, minced

2 tablespoons fresh dill, chopped

Preheat oven to 375 degrees F. Line a rimmed baking sheet with foil and coat lightly with nonstick cooking spray.

Place salmon on prepared baking sheet and season with salt and pepper to taste. Fold up foil around all four edges of the salmon, creating a basket.

In a small bowl, whisk together butter, the juice of one lemon, the zest of one lemon, garlic, and dill. Spoon butter mixture evenly over the salmon.

Thinly slice remaining lemon and top salmon with evenly spaced slices. Fold foil over the salmon and seal the packet.

Bake until cooked through, about 15 to 20 minutes.

Serve with Lemon Zoodles (page 141) and Parmesan Orzo (page 158).

COCONUT-CRUSTED TILAPIA

Prep time: 10 minutes | Cook time: 15 minutes | Total time: 25 minutes | Serves: 6

¼ **cup shredded unsweetened coconut**

¼ **cup Italian bread crumbs**

¼ **cup crushed Whole Wheat Ritz Crackers**

3 eggs, beaten

6 (4-ounce) tilapia fillets

Preheat oven to 400 degrees F. Line a rimmed baking sheet with foil and coat with nonstick cooking spray.

In a small, shallow bowl, toss together the coconut, bread crumbs, and crackers. Pour beaten eggs in a separate shallow bowl and mix to combine.

Dip each tilapia fillet in the egg and then dredge in the coconut-crumb mixture. Place fillets on prepared baking sheet and bake 15 minutes, until fish flakes easily and coconut-crumb mixture is golden brown.

Serve with Parmesan Lemon Asparagus (page 126) and Mushroom and Garlic Quinoa Bake (page 138).

GRILLED TILAPIA TACOS

Prep time: 15 minutes | Cook time: 10 minutes | Total time: 25 minutes | Serves: About 6 (2 tacos per person)

1 to 2 pounds tilapia fillets

12 corn tortillas

3 ripe tomatoes, seeded and diced

1 bunch cilantro, chopped

1 small head cabbage, cored and shredded

¼ cup Cilantro Avocado Dressing

Heat grill to medium high.

Season fish fillets with salt and pepper and place on hot grill. Cook until fish easily flakes with a fork, turning once, about 9 minutes. Remove fish from grill and chop or tear into bite-sized pieces.

Assemble tacos by placing a few spoonsful of fish pieces on one side of each tortilla. Top fish with tomatoes, cilantro, and cabbage; drizzle with dressing. To serve, fold up tortilla around fillings.

Serve with Caramelized Grilled Pineapple (page 145) and Italian Roasted Vegetable Medley (page 129).

main dishes

MANGO-CHILI SHRIMP

Prep time: 15 minutes | Cook time: 10 minutes | Total time: 25 minutes | Serves: 4

2 large mangoes, peeled and diced

¾ cup chili sauce

1 tablespoon lime juice

1 tablespoon honey

⅓ cup fresh, chopped cilantro

1 pound large shrimp, peeled and deveined

In a blender or a food processor, combine mangoes, chili sauce, lime juice, honey, and cilantro.

In a medium bowl, stir together shrimp and ½ cup of the mango salsa. Let sit 10 minutes in the refrigerator to marinate.

Remove shrimp and discard the marinade.

Skewer shrimp and grill 2 to 3 minutes per side over high heat until shrimp turn pink and opaque. Serve with remaining mango salsa.

Serve with Parmesan Orzo (page 158) and Caramelized Grilled Pineapple (page 145).

EASY LEMON GARLIC SHRIMP

Prep time: 5 minutes | Cook time: 10 minutes | Total time: 15 minutes

1 (16-ounce) package angel hair pasta

¼ cup butter, divided

4 teaspoons minced garlic

2 pounds large shrimp, peeled and deveined

Salt and pepper, to taste

2 tablespoons lemon juice

Cook pasta according to package directions; set aside.

Melt 2 tablespoons of the butter in a large skillet over medium heat.

Add garlic and sauté 30 seconds, until garlic is fragrant. Add shrimp and season with salt and pepper to taste. Cook shrimp, stirring occasionally, 5 to 6 minutes, or until pink and cooked through.

Off the heat, stir in lemon juice and remaining butter until butter is melted and everything is well combined.

Serve over cooked pasta, garnished with fresh parsley, if desired.

Serve with Roasted Balsamic Carrots (page 122) and Parmesan Orzo (page 158).

EASY CRAB CAKES

Prep time: 20 minutes | Cook time: 10 minutes | Total time: 30 minutes | Serves: 4

2 eggs

2 tablespoons mayonnaise

2 teaspoons Dijon mustard

1 pound fresh lump crab meat

2 tablespoons chopped green onions

½ cup bread crumbs

Preheat oven to 400 degrees F. Brush a baking sheet generously with olive oil.

In a medium mixing bowl, beat the eggs until foamy. Whip in the mayonnaise and mustard, and then gently fold in the crab meat, onions, and bread crumbs. Season with salt and pepper to taste.

Gently shape the mixture into four 1-inch-thick round patties and place on prepared pan. Bake 15 to 20 minutes, or until the tops are dry and lightly browned. Remove from oven and serve.

Serve with Watermelon Feta Salad (page 146) and Parmesan Orzo (page 158).

TUNA LETTUCE WRAPS

Prep time: 10 minutes | Total time: 10 minutes | Serves: 3

1 (5-ounce) can tuna

1 tablespoon sweet relish

1 tablespoon Miracle Whip or mayonnaise

1 teaspoon Dijon mustard

½ teaspoon lemon juice

3 large lettuce leaves

Combine tuna, relish, Miracle Whip or mayo, Dijon mustard, and lemon juice in a bowl, until well combined. Season with salt and pepper to taste. Place the mixture on a lettuce leaf and serve. This tastes great as is or topped with your favorite fresh veggies, such as diced tomatoes and bell peppers, or sliced avocado.

Serve with Watermelon Feta Salad (page 146) and Caramelized Grilled Pineapple (page 145).

RAVIOLI LASAGNA

Prep time: 10 minutes | Cook time: 40 minutes | Total time: 50 minutes | Serves: 6

1 (24-ounce) jar pasta sauce

1 (25-ounce) package frozen ravioli

1½ cups shredded mozzarella cheese

½ cup shredded Parmesan cheese

Chopped fresh basil, for topping

Preheat oven to 375 degrees F. Coat a 9x9-inch baking pan with cooking spray.

Pour ⅓ of the pasta sauce in the bottom of the pan. Top with half the ravioli, another third of the pasta sauce, and half the mozzarella cheese.

Repeat layers, then top with shredded Parmesan cheese.

Cover with foil and bake 30 minutes. Remove from the oven, uncover, and bake an additional 10 minutes, or until cheese is melted and starts to brown. Sprinkle with chopped fresh basil and serve warm.

Serve with Italian Roasted Vegetable Medley (page 129) and Easy Homemade Rolls (page 166).

EASY BAKED GNOCCHI

Prep time: 5 minutes | Cook time: 15 minutes | Total time: 20 minutes | Serves: 6

1½ pounds premade potato gnocchi

½ cup coarsely chopped fresh basil

1 (26-ounce) jar marinara sauce

1 to 2 cups shredded mozzarella cheese

Preheat oven to 425 degrees F. Coat a 9x13-inch baking dish with nonstick cooking spray and set aside.

Carefully place gnocchi in a large pot of salted, boiling water. When the gnocchi float to the top of the pot, remove with a slotted spoon and place in the prepared baking dish. Sprinkle basil on top of the gnocchi and carefully spoon marinara sauce evenly on top of the basil. Sprinkle cheese evenly over the sauce.

Bake 15 minutes. Allow to cool for a few minutes before serving. Garnish with additional basil, if desired.

Serve with Italian Roasted Vegetable Medley (page 129) and One-Pan Triple-Berry Cobbler (page 201).

EASY CAPRESE PASTA BAKE

Prep time: 15 minutes | Cook time: 30 minutes | Total time: 45 minutes | Serves: 8

1 (16-ounce) box penne pasta

1½ cups halved cherry tomatoes

2 tablespoons chopped, fresh basil

1¼ cups chicken broth, divided

10 to 12 ounces fresh mozzarella cheese

1 tablespoon balsamic vinegar

Preheat oven to 375 degrees F.

In a large pot over high heat, bring 6 cups water to a boil. Add noodles and boil for 5 minutes, then run under cold water to stop additional cooking. Drain.

In a bowl, combine cooked noodles, tomatoes, basil, and 1 cup chicken broth. Crumble enough of the fresh mozzarella to make about ½ cup of crumbles and then stir into the noodle mixture.

Pour remaining ¼ cup chicken broth in the bottom of a 9x13-inch pan. Add noodle mixture and spread evenly in pan. Slice remaining mozzarella cheese and layer over the top.

Drizzle top of casserole with balsamic vinegar and, if desired, a small amount of extra virgin olive oil. Bake 30 minutes, or until cheese begins to bubble and turn golden brown.

Serve with Fresh Berry Salad (page 149) and Easy Homemade Rolls (page 166).

CAPRESE TOAST

Prep time: 15 minutes | Total time: 15 minutes | Serves: 6

6 slices whole wheat bread

2 cloves garlic, peeled and cut in half

12 ounces fresh mozzarella cheese, sliced ¼-inch thick

1 bunch fresh basil leaves

1 cup halved cherry tomatoes

3 tablespoons balsamic glaze

Toast bread slices. Use the cut side of a garlic clove to liberally rub the garlic over one side of a slice of toast. Repeat, using remaining garlic and toast slices.

Place 1 to 2 pieces of mozzarella on each piece of toast, and then top with some tomatoes and a few basil leaves. Drizzle with balsamic glaze. Alternatively, you can drizzle with extra virgin olive oil, salt, and pepper or use all three in addition to the balsamic glaze.

Serve with Parmesan Lemon Asparagus (page 126) and Layered Strawberry Jell-O (page 150).

PORTOBELLO FAJITAS

Prep time: 10 minutes | Cook time: 15 minutes | Total time: 25 minutes | Serves: 4 (2 fajitas per person)

2 bell peppers, sliced thin

½ onion, sliced thin

1 tablespoon extra virgin olive oil

2 medium portobello mushrooms, sliced thin

1 (1-ounce) packet fajita seasoning

8 small flour tortillas

In a nonstick skillet over medium heat, sauté bell peppers and onions in olive oil 2 to 3 minutes. Add in portobello mushrooms and fajita seasoning. Stir and continue cooking until peppers and onions are tender, about 8 to 10 minutes.

Spoon the mixture into tortillas and serve warm with your favorite fajita toppings, such as fresh lime juice, sour cream, shredded cheese, guacamole, and salsa.

Serve with Texas Pinto Beans (page 162) and Green Chile Rice (page 161).

ENCHILADA QUINOA

Prep time: 10 minutes | Cook time: 1 hour 30 minutes | Total time: 1 hour 40 minutes | Serves: 4

1 cup uncooked quinoa

1 can black beans, drained and rinsed

1 can corn, drained

1 tablespoon minced garlic

1 (1-ounce) packet taco seasoning

2 cups red enchilada sauce

In a slow cooker, combine the quinoa, black beans, corn, garlic, taco seasoning, and enchilada sauce. Stir until fully incorporated. Cook on high 1 hour and 30 minutes, or until quinoa is soft. Before serving, season with salt and pepper to taste. For more flavor, you can also add half an onion (diced) or a teaspoon of cumin powder before cooking.

Remove from slow cooker. Serve immediately, topped with your favorite meat or enchilada toppings, if desired.

Serve with Texas Pinto Beans (page 162) and Muddy Buddies (page 193).

WHITE-BEAN TUSCAN SKILLET

Prep time: 5 minutes | Cook time: 35 minutes | Total time: 40 minutes | Serves: 4

---

8 ounces cremini mushrooms, sliced

1½ cups diced yellow onion

3 cloves garlic, minced

⅔ cup drained and chopped oil-packed sun-dried tomatoes

2 (14.5-ounce) cans fire-roasted diced tomatoes

2 (14.5-ounce) cans cannellini beans, drained and rinsed

Heat a small amount of olive oil in a large skillet over medium-high heat until oil begins to ripple. Add the mushrooms and brown 3 to 4 minutes. You may need to do this in 2 batches, depending on the size of your skillet.

Transfer mushrooms to a medium bowl. Add a little more olive oil to the skillet and heat until oil ripples. Sauté onions in oil until lightly browned, about 5 minutes. Stir in the garlic and sun-dried tomatoes and cook until softened, another 2 minutes.

Stir in the diced tomatoes and beans and season with salt and pepper, to taste. Reduce heat to medium, cover pan, and cook 10 minutes. Return mushrooms to the pan, stir, and cook for another minute or 2 to warm them up. Serve hot with a good crusty bread for dipping and scooping up the beans.

Serve with Green Beans with Candied Pecans (page 121) and Greek Yogurt Fruit Salad (page 153).

side dishes

GREEN BEANS WITH CANDIED PECANS

Prep time: 10 minutes | Cook time: 10 minutes | Total time: 20 minutes | Serves: 6 to 8

2 pounds fresh green beans, trimmed

1 cup chopped pecans

¼ cup packed brown sugar

2 tablespoons butter

Salt and pepper, to taste

Bring 4 quarts water to boil in a large pot over medium heat. Fill a large bowl with ice water and place a colander in the bowl; set aside.

Cook beans in hot water for exactly 5 minutes. Use a slotted spoon to transfer beans to the colander in ice water. This will immediately stop the cooking so beans remain a vibrant green color and are crisp-tender. Drain well.

In a large skillet over medium high heat, continuously stir pecans and brown sugar until the sugar is completely melted and pecans are evenly coated. Spread candied pecans in an even layer on waxed paper or a baking sheet until cool. Once cool, break apart into smaller pieces if necessary.

Melt butter in a large skillet over medium heat, add beans, and sauté until heated through, about 2 minutes. Season with salt and pepper. Top with candied pecans. Serve immediately.

Serve with Savory Slow-Cooker Turkey Breast (page 43) or Grilled Pork Loin Medallions (page 75).

ROASTED BALSAMIC CARROTS

Prep time: 5 minutes | Cook time: 25 minutes | Total time: 30 minutes

1 (16-ounce) bag baby carrots

2 tablespoons olive oil

2 tablespoons balsamic vinegar

Salt and pepper, to taste

Preheat oven to 450 degrees F.

Layer baby carrots evenly in the bottom of an 8x8-inch baking dish. Drizzle balsamic vinegar and 1 tablespoon of the olive oil over the carrots and toss to coat. Sprinkle with salt and pepper to taste and bake 15 minutes.

Remove dish from oven and drizzle remaining olive oil over carrots. Return dish to oven and bake an additional 10 to 15 minutes, until carrots are tender and begin to turn brown around the edges. (A longer cooking time will result in softer carrots.)

Serve with Avocado Chicken Bites (page 40) or Easy Lemon Garlic Shrimp (page 99).

PARMESAN PEAS

Prep time: 5 minutes | Cook time: 10 minutes | Total time: 15 minutes | Serves: 6

2 tablespoons extra virgin olive oil

2 tablespoons diced onions

1 (14-ounce) bag frozen peas

½ teaspoon salt

2 tablespoons freshly squeezed lemon juice

¼ cup grated Parmesan cheese

Heat the oil in a large skillet over medium-high heat until oil ripples. Add onions and cook until they turn soft and translucent, about 6 to 7 minutes.

Stir in the peas and salt and cook about 3 minutes, or until peas are barely soft. Remove from heat. Stir in lemon juice, and top with Parmesan cheese and freshly ground black pepper, if desired. Serve immediately.

Serve with Grilled Mediterranean Pork Kabobs (page 76) or Chicken-Parmesan Pasta Casserole (page 36).

PARMESAN LEMON ASPARAGUS

Prep time: 5 minutes | Cook time: 20 minutes | Total time: 25 minutes | Serves: 4

1 bunch asparagus

1 tablespoon extra virgin olive oil

1½ tablespoons grated Parmesan cheese, plus extra for topping

1 lemon

Preheat oven to 375 degrees F.

Wash and chop asparagus into bite-sized pieces, discarding the tough, white ends.

Spread asparagus on a rimmed baking sheet and toss in olive oil and Parmesan cheese. Cut lemon in half and juice 1 half over the asparagus; toss again. Bake 10 to 15 minutes, or until asparagus is crisp-tender and cheese begins to turn golden brown.

Squeeze juice from the other half of the lemon over the top and garnish with additional Parmesan cheese. Serve immediately.

Serve with Chicken-Parmesan Pasta Casserole (page 36) or Easy Baked Gnocchi (page 107).

ITALIAN ROASTED VEGETABLE MEDLEY

Prep time: 5 minutes | Cook time: 20 minutes | Total time: 25 minutes | Serves: 6 to 8

3 cups broccoli florets

3 cups cauliflower florets

3 cups baby carrots

2 tablespoons extra virgin olive oil

1 tablespoon dry zesty Italian dressing mix

1 tablespoon shredded Parmesan cheese

Preheat oven to 425 degrees F.

Spread broccoli, cauliflower, and carrots on a large baking sheet. Drizzle olive oil over vegetables. Sprinkle on Italian dressing mix and shredded Parmesan. Toss vegetables with hands until evenly coated in oil and seasoning. Bake 20 minutes, or until vegetables are tender.

Serve with Grilled Mediterranean Pork Kabobs (page 76) or Maple-Pecan Pork Tenderloin (page 67).

MAPLE-ROASTED BUTTERNUT SQUASH

Prep time: 5 minutes | Cook time: 25 minutes | Total time: 30 minutes | Serves: 6

6 cups peeled and cubed butternut squash

1 tablespoon extra virgin olive oil

2 tablespoons real maple syrup

¼ teaspoon ground cinnamon

Salt and pepper, to taste

Preheat oven to 400 degrees F. Line a rimmed baking sheet with foil or parchment paper and coat lightly with nonstick cooking spray.

Spread squash in an even layer on prepared pan and drizzle olive oil and maple syrup over the top. Sprinkle with cinnamon and salt and pepper to taste.

Toss squash with hands until pieces are completely coated in oil, syrup, and seasonings. Bake 20 to 25 minutes or until squash is golden brown on the outside and tender on the inside.

Serve with Coconut-Crusted Tilapia (page 92) or Creamy Mustard Pork Chops (page 83).

SLOW COOKER CREAMED CORN

Prep time: 5 minutes | Cook time: 4 hours | Total time: 4 hours 5 minutes | Serves: 8 to 10

2 (16-ounce) bags frozen corn kernels

1 (8-ounce) brick cream cheese

½ cup (1 stick) butter

½ cup milk

1 tablespoon granulated sugar

Chopped fresh thyme, for garnishing

Place corn, cream cheese, butter, milk, and sugar in a slow cooker and season with salt and pepper, to taste. Cover and cook on high 2 to 4 hours or low 4 to 6 hours.

Remove lid and stir to combine. Garnish with fresh thyme before serving.

Serve with One-Pan Sausage and Tortellini (page 84) or Creamy Turkey-Zucchini Casserole (page 56).

TWICE-BAKED BACON-AND-CHIVE SWEET POTATOES

Prep time: 15 minutes | Cook time: 1 hour 15 minutes | Total time: 1 hour 30 minutes | Serves: 4

2 sweet potatoes

½ cup sour cream

4 slices bacon, cooked and crumbled

¼ cup milk

1 tablespoon dried chives

1 cup shredded cheddar cheese

Preheat oven to 350 degrees F.

Stab each potato with the tines of a fork 4 to 5 times and bake directly on hot oven rack for 1 hour.

When potatoes are done, allow them to cool 10 minutes. Slice potatoes in half lengthwise and scoop the flesh into a large bowl. Place empty skins on a rimmed baking sheet and set aside.

Add sour cream, milk, bacon, chives, ½ cup of the cheese, and salt and pepper to taste to the sweet potato flesh and mix with an electric hand mixer on low speed until creamy.

Spoon the mixture into the potato skins. Top with remaining shredded cheese and return to the oven to bake 15 minutes, until cheese is browned and bubbly. If desired, top with extra bacon and more chives.

Serve with Savory Slow-Cooker Turkey Breast (page 43) or Fall-Apart Slow Cooker Roast (page 3).

CRANBERRY-PECAN SWEET POTATO BAKE

Prep time: 10 minutes | Cook time: 40 minutes | Total time: 50 minutes | Serves: 8 to 10

¾ cup butter (1½ sticks), melted

⅓ cup packed brown sugar

2 tablespoons honey

3 to 4 medium-sized sweet potatoes, peeled and sliced into ¼-inch-thick rounds

1½ cups dried cranberries

1 cup chopped pecans

Preheat oven to 400 degrees F. Coat a 9x13-inch pan with nonstick cooking spray.

In a small bowl, combine the melted butter, brown sugar, and honey. Mix until fully incorporated.

Layer half of the potato slices on the bottom of the prepared pan. (Do not stack potato rounds on top of each other.) Top potatoes with a little less than half of the brown-sugar mixture, spreading it evenly over sweet potatoes. Sprinkle half of the dried cranberries and half of the pecans over that.

Repeat layers, finishing off by drizzling the last of the brown-sugar-and-butter mixture over the top.

Bake, uncovered, 35 to 40 minutes, until sweet potatoes are cooked through and the tops have turned a nice golden brown.

Serve with Savory Slow-Cooker Turkey Breast (page 43) or Cranberry Slow-Cooker Turkey Breast (page 44) and Golden Grahams S'mores Bars (page 176) for dessert.

MUSHROOM AND GARLIC QUINOA BAKE

Prep time: 10 minutes | Cook time: 15 minutes | Total time: 25 minutes | Serves: 4 to 6

---

1 cup uncooked quinoa

1 pound cremini mushrooms, sliced

2 tablespoons minced garlic

1½ tablespoons extra virgin olive oil

1 teaspoon paprika

⅓ cup freshly grated Parmesan cheese

Cook quinoa according to package directions.

While quinoa cooks, heat oil in a large skillet over medium-high heat until oil starts to ripple. Add mushrooms and garlic to the hot oil and sauté until the mushrooms soften, about 10 minutes.

In a large bowl, combine cooked quinoa, paprika, Parmesan cheese, and salt and pepper to taste. Mix well. Stir in mushrooms and serve warm.

Serve with Pineapple Chicken Tenders (page 27) or Brown-Sugar-Glazed Pork Chops (page 79).

LEMON ZOODLES

Prep time: 5 minutes | Cook time: 10 minutes | Total time: 15 minutes | Serves: 4

2 tablespoons extra virgin olive oil

1 teaspoon minced garlic

12 ounces fresh or frozen zucchini noodles

Grated Parmesan cheese, to taste

Zest and juice of one lemon

1 tablespoon freshly chopped basil

Heat olive oil in a large skillet over medium heat. Stir in minced garlic and stir until fragrant, about 30 seconds, being careful not to cook garlic too long by itself, as it can easily scorch.

Add in zucchini noodles, then cover and cook 10 minutes for frozen noodles and 2 to 3 minutes for fresh noodles, stirring occasionally. Remove from heat, drain excess liquid if necessary, and stir in Parmesan cheese, ½ tablespoon lemon zest, lemon juice, and basil. Serve warm.

Serve with Baked Saltine-Cracker Chicken (page 24) or Coconut-Crusted Tilapia (page 92).

APPLE CARROT SLAW

Prep time: 15 minutes | Total time: 15 minutes | Serves: 8

5 medium carrots, peeled and grated

2 honeycrisp apples, diced

1 cup dried cranberries

½ cup mayonnaise (do not use Miracle Whip)

2 teaspoons freshly squeezed lemon juice

1 tablespoon granulated sugar

In a large bowl, toss together carrots, apples, and dried cranberries. In a separate, small bowl, whisk together mayonnaise, lemon juice, and sugar, and then pour over carrot mixture. Stir well. Chill, covered, in the refrigerator until ready to serve.

Serve with Barbecue Turkey Burgers (page 60) or Taco Stuffed Peppers (page 11).

CARAMELIZED GRILLED PINEAPPLE

Prep time: 30 minutes | Cook time: 15 minutes | Total time: 45 minutes | Serves: 8

1 pineapple, cored and cut into large wedges

¼ cup packed brown sugar

¼ cup (½ stick) butter, melted

½ teaspoon cinnamon

½ teaspoon vanilla extract

1 tablespoon honey

Heat grill to medium-high heat.

If using wooden skewers, soak skewers in water at least 30 minutes before threading on pineapple. Thread pineapple onto skewers.

In a small bowl, mix together brown sugar, butter, cinnamon, vanilla, and honey. Place pineapple skewers on a large plate or pan. Brush brown-sugar glaze liberally and evenly over each piece of pineapple. Place skewers on hot grill and cook 5 to 7 minutes on each side, or just until the sugar-glaze starts to caramelize. Serve warm as a delicious appetizer, side dish, or dessert.

Serve with Grilled Pork Loin Medallions (page 75) or Smoky Slow-Cooker Pulled Pork (page 68).

WATERMELON FETA SALAD

Prep time: 10 minutes | Total time: 10 minutes | Serves: 4

3 cups cubed watermelon

1 cup diced cucumbers

1 cup crumbled feta

¼ cup thinly sliced red onion

½ cup freshly chopped mint

Balsamic vinegar (optional)

In a large bowl, toss together watermelon, cucumbers, feta, red onion slices, and mint. Drizzle with balsamic vinegar to taste, if desired.

Serve with Turkey Club Roll-Ups (page 51) or Tuna Lettuce Wraps (page 103).

FRESH BERRY SALAD

Prep time: 15 minutes | Total time: 15 minutes | Serves: 8

2 cups quartered strawberries

1½ cups blueberries

1½ cups blackberries

1½ cups raspberries

1 tablespoon apple juice

Zest and juice of 1 lime

Toss together strawberries, blueberries, blackberries, raspberries, and apple juice in a large bowl. Toss berries with lime juice and sprinkle top with zest. Refrigerate until cold, about 2 hours, and then serve.

Serve with Grilled Mediterranean Pork Kabobs (page 76) or Barbecue Turkey Burgers (page 60).

LAYERED STRAWBERRY JELL-O

Prep time: 20 minutes | Chilling time: 3 hours 10 minutes | Total time: 3 hours 30 minutes | Serves: 9

1 (6-ounce) box strawberry Jell-O

1½ cups boiling water

1 (8-ounce) can crushed pineapple, drained

2 ripe bananas, mashed to remove all lumps

20 strawberries, thinly sliced and divided

1 cup sour cream

In a medium bowl, stir together Jell-O and boiling water 2 to 3 minutes, until Jell-O is completely dissolved.

Stir in crushed pineapple, mashed bananas, and a little more than half of the sliced strawberries; set aside.

In a small bowl, stir sour cream until very smooth, creamy, and spreadable.

Pour half of the Jell-O and fruit mixture into a 9x13-inch baking dish. Freeze 5 to 10 minutes, just to let Jell-O set a little.

Carefully ladle the sour cream over the Jell-O and spread in an even layer.

Carefully and evenly pour remaining Jell-O and fruit mixture over the sour cream. Layer the rest of the sliced strawberries on top. Cover and refrigerate at least 3 hours.

Serve with Parmesan Peas (page 125) and Barbecue Biscuit Cups (page 16).

GREEK YOGURT FRUIT SALAD

Prep time: 10 minutes | Total time: 10 minutes | Serves: 6

1 (20-ounce) can pineapple tidbits, drained well

1 (11-ounce) can mandarin oranges, drained well

1½ cups sliced strawberries

1½ cups blueberries

1½ cups blackberries

2 (5.3-ounce) cartons vanilla Greek yogurt

In a large bowl, gently toss fruit together and then fold in Greek yogurt. Try experimenting with your favorite fruits if you don't like one or more of those listed above. Grapes, banana slices, kiwi slices, and raspberries are all good options. Serve immediately or store in refrigerator up to 5 hours before serving. The fruit tends to make the salad watery if stored much longer than that. Serve and enjoy!

Serve with Barbecue Chicken Tostadas (page 32) or Taco Crescent Rolls (page 15).

BROWN-SUGAR FRUIT DIP

Prep time: 5 minutes | Total time: 5 minutes | Serves: 6 to 8

1 (8-ounce) brick cream cheese, softened
½ cup packed brown sugar
1 tablespoon vanilla extract

In a small bowl, combine cream cheese, brown sugar, and vanilla. Use an electric mixer to beat until smooth. Serve with strawberries, sliced apples, bananas slices, or any fruit of your choosing.

Serve with Taco Crescent Rolls (page 15) or Crispy Steak Burritos (page 7).

POMEGRANATE SALSA

Prep time: 5 minutes | Total time: 5 minutes | Serves: 6

1 cup pomegranate arils

1 jalapeño, diced and seeded

⅓ cup diced fresh cilantro

½ small red onion, diced

Juice from 1 lime

Pinch cumin

Combine all ingredients in a small bowl. Season with salt and pepper, to taste, and serve with tortilla chips or crackers.

Serve with Turkey Taco Meatballs (page 59) or Citrus and Onion Pulled Pork Sliders (page 71).

side dishes

PARMESAN ORZO

Prep time: 10 minutes | Cook time: 10 minutes | Total time: 20 minutes | Serves: 4

2 tablespoons butter

1 cup uncooked orzo pasta

1 (14.5-ounce) can chicken broth

½ cup grated Parmesan cheese

1 tablespoon dried basil

Salt and pepper, to taste

In a large skillet over medium-high heat, melt butter until it begins to foam. Add orzo and sauté until lightly browned, about 3 to 5 minutes.

Stir in chicken stock and bring to a boil. Reduce heat to a simmer, cover, and let it cook, stirring occasionally, until liquid is absorbed and orzo is tender, about 10 to 12 minutes.

Stir in Parmesan cheese, basil, and salt and pepper to taste. Serve warm.

Serve with Pesto Salmon (page 88) or Grilled Mediterranean Pork Kabobs (page 76).

GREEN CHILE RICE

Prep time: 15 minutes | Cook time: 20 minutes | Total time: 35 minutes | Serves: 8

4 cups cooked white rice

2 cups shredded mozzarella cheese

2 cups sour cream

1 (4-ounce) can diced green chiles, drained

Preheat oven to 400 degrees F. Grease an 8x8-inch baking dish.

In a large bowl, combine all ingredients and mix well. Transfer to prepared baking dish and bake 20 minutes, until heated through and bubbly.

Serve with Turkey Taco Lettuce Wraps (page 48) or Grilled Tilapia Tacos (page 95).

TEXAS PINTO BEANS

Prep time: 5 minutes | Cook time: 10 to 15 minutes | Total time: 20 minutes | Serves: 6

1 onion, diced

2 teaspoons freshly chopped cilantro

1 clove garlic, minced

2 (15-ounce) cans pinto beans, drained and rinsed

¾ cup salsa

½ teaspoon cumin

Heat a small amount of olive oil in a large skillet over medium-high heat until oil begins to ripple. Add onions and cilantro and sauté until onions are tender, about 6 to 7 minutes. Stir in garlic and cook 1 minute longer.

Stir in the beans, salsa, and cumin and heat through.

If desired, top warm beans with cheese and sour cream.

Serve with Oven-Baked Chicken Tacos (page 35) or Taco Crescent Rolls (page 15).

CHEESY PULL-APART BISCUITS

Prep time: 5 minutes | Cook time: 12 minutes | Total time: 17 minutes | Makes: 12 biscuits

1 (16-ounce) package refrigerated biscuit dough

½ teaspoon garlic powder

3 tablespoons extra virgin olive oil

1⅓ cups shredded cheddar cheese

1½ tablespoons freshly chopped parsley

1½ tablespoons grated Parmesan cheese

Preheat oven to 350 degrees F. Coat a 12-cup muffin tin with nonstick cooking spray.

Cut each biscuit into fourths and place them in a large mixing bowl. Sprinkle on garlic powder, olive oil, cheddar cheese, and parsley and toss gently.

Place 3 to 4 biscuit pieces in each muffin cup and sprinkle with Parmesan cheese. Bake 11 to 14 minutes, until biscuits are golden brown on top.

Serve with Ravioli Lasagna (page 104) or Fall-Apart Slow Cooker Roast (page 3).

EASY HOMEMADE ROLLS

Prep Time: 5 hours 10 minutes | Cook Time: 10 minutes | Total Time: 5 hours 20 minutes | Makes: 32 rolls

1 tablespoon active dry yeast

½ cup granulated sugar

3 eggs, beaten

½ cup melted butter

½ teaspoon salt

4 cups all-purpose flour

In a large bowl, dissolve yeast in 1 cup lukewarm water. Let mixture rest 5 minutes, until yeast is activated and foamy.

With a wooden spoon, stir in sugar, beaten eggs, butter, and salt. Fold in all-purpose flour and mix well. Cover the bowl with plastic wrap and allow dough to rise 4 to 6 hours on the countertop or overnight in the refrigerator. Do not knead the dough.

Preheat oven to 375 degrees F.

Turn out dough on a lightly floured surface and divide in half. Roll each half into a ⅛-inch-thick circle. Brush each circle with additional melted butter and cut into 16 wedges.

Roll up each wedge from the large end to the point. Place rolls on a baking sheet, cover with plastic wrap, and let rise 30 to 60 minutes, until rolls are doubled in size. Bake 8 to 10 minutes, until tops are golden brown.

Serve with Fall-Apart Slow Cooker Roast (page 3) or Slow Cooker Root-Beer-Glazed Ribs (page 72).

desserts

NO-BAKE PEANUT BUTTER CORN FLAKE BARS

Prep time: 5 minutes | Cook time: 10 minutes | Total time: 15 minutes | Makes: About 12 bars

½ cup granulated sugar

½ cup light corn syrup

1 cup creamy peanut butter

3 cups crushed corn flakes

2 cups milk chocolate chips

Grease a 9x13-inch pan or coat with nonstick cooking spray.

In a large saucepan over medium heat, cook sugar and corn syrup together, stirring constantly, until it begins to boil.

Remove from heat and stir in peanut butter until completely melted. Stir in crushed corn flakes and then press mixture into prepared pan.

In a microwave-safe bowl, microwave chocolate chips on high power in 30-second increments until smooth and melted, stirring between each interval. Spread chocolate on top of cereal mixture.

Let cool until firm, and then cut into squares and serve.

SAMOA BROWNIES

Prep time: 15 minutes | Cook time: 55 minutes | Total time: 1 hour 10 minutes | Makes: 9 brownies

3½ cups shredded coconut

2 (13-ounce) bags Kraft Caramels, unwrapped

½ teaspoon salt

¼ cup milk

1 (18-ounce) box brownie mix, baked according to package directions and cooled

3 ounces semisweet chocolate, melted

Preheat oven to 400 degrees F.

Spread coconut evenly on a rimmed baking sheet. Cook 2 to 3 minutes. Remove from oven, stir, and return to oven another 2 to 3 minutes. Toast until coconut is fragrant and golden brown. Watch closely so it doesn't burn. Set aside to cool.

Place unwrapped caramels, salt, and milk in a large, microwave-safe bowl and cook in microwave on high power 3 to 5 minutes, stopping to stir every 45 to 60 seconds, until caramels are melted and mixture is smooth.

Add coconut to caramel and mix together. Spread mixture over cooled brownies. Refrigerate 4 to 5 hours or overnight.

Remove brownies from refrigerator at least 1 hour before cutting. Cut into bars and drizzle each bar with some melted semisweet chocolate.

NO-BAKE COCONUT BARS

Prep time: 10 minutes | Time in freezer: 1 hour | Total time: 1 hour 10 minutes | Makes: 9 bars

2½ cups sweetened, flaked coconut

1 cup coconut oil, melted

2 teaspoons vanilla extract

½ teaspoon salt

¾ cup dark chocolate chips

In a medium bowl, mix together coconut, coconut oil, vanilla, and salt until well combined. Spread mixture into a 9x9-inch baking dish and freeze until coconut oil has set and bars harden, about 30 minutes.

In a microwave-safe bowl, microwave chocolate chips on high power in 30-second increments until smooth and melted, stirring between each interval. Pour chocolate over coconut. Freeze another 30 minutes, or until chocolate has set up.

Cut into bars and serve.

GOLDEN GRAHAMS S'MORES BARS

Prep time: 12 minutes | Cooling time: 15 to 20 minutes | Total time: 27 to 32 minutes | Makes: 12 to 15 bars

8 cups Golden Grahams cereal

6 cups miniature marshmallows, divided

1½ cups milk chocolate chips

¼ cup light corn syrup

5 tablespoons butter or margarine

1 teaspoon vanilla extract

Pour cereal into a large bowl and set aside. Coat a 9x13-inch baking dish with nonstick cooking spray.

In a large, microwave-safe bowl, microwave 5 cups of marshmallows, chocolate chips, corn syrup, and butter on high power 2 to 3 minutes, stirring after each minute, until mixture is smooth and all ingredients are melted. Stir in vanilla.

Pour mixture over cereal and quickly toss until cereal is completely coated. Stir in remaining 1 cup marshmallows.

Press mixture evenly into pan and let rest, uncovered, until cool. Refrigerate if you prefer a firmer bar. Cut into bars and serve. Store loosely covered at room temperature up to 2 days.

CHEWY CHEX BARS

Prep time: 20 minutes | Total time: 20 minutes | Makes: About 15 bars

¼ cup (½ stick) butter

4 cups miniature marshmallows

8 cups Rice Chex cereal

2 cups M&M's candies

½ cup milk chocolate chips

Coat a 9x13-inch baking dish with nonstick cooking spray.

In a large, microwave-safe bowl, melt butter and marshmallows together on high power in 30-second increments, stirring between each interval, until mixture is smooth. Fold in Rice Chex and M&M's and mix well. Press mixture evenly into prepared baking dish.

In a small, microwave-safe bowl, microwave chocolate chips on high power in 30-second increments, stirring between each interval, until chips are melted and smooth. Use a spoon to gently drizzle melted chocolate over the Chex Bars. Let cool 10 minutes, slice into bars, and serve. If not serving immediately, cool in refrigerator.

STRAWBERRY CRINKLE COOKIES

Prep time: 10 minutes | Cook time: 9 minutes | Total time: 19 minutes | Makes: 24 to 30 cookies

1 (15.25-ounce) box strawberry cake mix

½ cup vegetable oil

2 large eggs

½ cup powdered sugar, for rolling the cookies in

Preheat oven to 350 degrees F.

In a large bowl, stir together the dry cake mix, oil, and eggs to form a thick dough.

Dust hands with powdered sugar and shape dough into 1-inch balls. Roll balls in powdered sugar and place 2 inches apart on an ungreased cookie sheet.

Bake for 7 to 9 minutes, until center is just barely set. Let cookies cool one minute on cookie sheet, then remove to a wire rack to finish cooling.

CAKE MIX M&M'S COOKIES

Prep time: 15 minutes | Cook time: 10 minutes | Total time: 25 minutes | Makes: 24 to 30 cookies

1 (15.25-ounce) box chocolate cake mix

⅓ cup vegetable oil

1 teaspoon vanilla extract

2 large eggs

1 cup M&M's chocolate candies

Preheat oven to 350 degrees F.

In a large bowl, mix together dry cake mix, vegetable oil, vanilla, and eggs to form a very thick dough. Fold in M&M's chocolate candies.

Roll the dough into 1-inch balls and place on an ungreased cookie sheet. Bake 9 to 11 minutes, until set and lightly browned. Let cookies cool 2 minutes on cookie sheet, then remove to a wire rack to finish cooling.

CAKE BATTER CHEESECAKE

Prep time: 40 minutes | Total time: 40 minutes | Serves: 8

1 cup heavy cream

1 (8-ounce) brick cream cheese, softened

⅔ cup Pillsbury Funfetti Premium Cake Mix

1 teaspoon vanilla extract

1 (9-inch) premade graham cracker crust

Sprinkles, for garnishing

In a large bowl with an electric mixer set to high speed, whip the cream until soft peaks form. Beat in cream cheese, cake mix, and vanilla until smooth and fully combined.

Pour the mixture into prepared graham cracker crust and top with sprinkles. Refrigerate 30 minutes to an hour before serving.

NUTTER-BUTTER COOKIE TRUFFLES

Prep time: 15 minutes | Freezing time: 40 to 45 minutes | Total time: 1 hour | Makes: 30 to 40 truffles

1 (16-ounce) package Nutter Butter Peanut Butter Sandwich Cookies

1 (8-ounce) brick cream cheese, cubed and at room temperature

1 (8-ounce) bag Reese's Peanut Butter Cups Minis, coarsely chopped

1 (12-ounce) bag milk chocolate chips

2 teaspoons shortening

1 tablespoon sprinkles (optional)

Line a rimmed baking sheet with parchment or waxed paper.

In the bowl of a food processor, blend Nutter Butter cookies to make fine crumbs. Add cubed cream cheese and process again to blend well.

Transfer mixture to a medium bowl and gently fold in Reese's Peanut Butter Cups Minis. Roll dough into 1-inch balls and place on prepared baking sheet. Freeze 30 to 40 minutes.

In a microwave-safe bowl, microwave chocolate chips and shortening on high power in 30-second increments until smooth and melted, stirring between each interval.

Remove truffles from freezer. Use a fork to pierce and pick up a frozen truffle. Dip the truffle into melted chocolate, making sure to cover truffle completely in chocolate. Lift up fork and gently tap it on the rim of the bowl to allow excess chocolate to drip back into the bowl. Return truffle to prepared baking sheet. If using sprinkles, immediately shake a few over the truffle. Repeat the process until all the truffles are covered in chocolate and sprinkles.

Let sit a few minutes before serving. Store leftover truffles in an airtight container in the refrigerator.

NO-BAKE LEMON COOKIE TRUFFLES

Prep time: 25 minutes | Chilling time: 1 hour 15 minutes | Total time: 1 hour 40 minutes | Makes: About 48 Truffles

1 (16-ounce) package lemon sandwich cookies

1 (8-ounce) brick cream cheese, softened

1 (16-ounce) package almond bark or white chocolate candy coating

Yellow jimmies or sprinkles (optional)

Line a baking sheet with parchment paper, waxed paper, or foil.

Crush cookies in the bowl of a food processor to make fine crumbs. Alternatively, put cookies in a resealable plastic bag, seal bag, and smash with a rolling pin to make fine crumbs.

Transfer cookie crumbs to a medium bowl. Add cream cheese and stir until well-blended. Roll cookie mixture into 1-inch balls and place balls on prepared pan. Freeze 45 minutes.

Just before removing truffles from freezer, melt almond bark according to package directions. Use a fork to pierce and pick up a frozen truffle. Dip the truffle into melted almond bark, making sure to cover truffle completely. Lift up fork and gently tap it on the rim of the bowl to allow excess almond bark to drip back into the bowl. Return truffle to prepared baking sheet. Top with yellow jimmies or sprinkles, if desired. Repeat with remaining truffles and then refrigerate 30 minutes to set almond bark.

Store leftover truffles in an airtight container in the refrigerator.

S'MORES FUDGE

Prep time: 10 minutes | Chilling time: 2 hours | Total time: 2 hours 10 minutes | Makes: 16 to 20 pieces fudge

1½ cups semisweet chocolate chips

⅔ cup sweetened condensed milk

2 teaspoons vanilla extract

1½ cups miniature marshmallows

3 whole graham crackers, broken into pieces

Coat an 8x8-inch baking dish with nonstick cooking spray.

In a microwave-safe bowl, microwave chocolate chips and sweetened condensed milk on high power 1 minute. Stir well to allow chocolate to melt completely.

Stir in vanilla and then fold in marshmallows and graham crackers pieces until just combined.

Pour mixture evenly into prepared pan and smooth out top. Refrigerate 2 hours, until set. Store leftover fudge in an airtight container in the refrigerator.

3-INGREDIENT M&M'S FUDGE

Prep time: 10 minutes | Cook time: 5 minutes | Total time: 15 minutes | Makes: 24 pieces fudge

1 (14-ounce) can sweetened condensed milk

1 (12-ounce) bag semisweet chocolate chips

1¼ cups M&M's Minis Baking Bits, divided

Line an 8-inch square baking dish with parchment paper, leaving 2 inches hanging over the ends.

In a saucepan over medium heat, cook and stir sweetened condensed milk and chocolate chips until chocolate is melted and mixture is smooth.

Remove from heat and stir in ¾ cup M&M's Minis Baking Bits.

Pour mixture into prepared baking dish, using a spatula to smooth out the top. Sprinkle remaining M&M's Minis Baking Bits over the top, pressing slightly into the mixture.

Cover with plastic wrap and refrigerate at least 2 hours. Cut into squares before serving. Store leftover fudge in an airtight container in the refrigerator.

MUDDY BUDDIES

Prep time: 15 to 20 minutes | Total time: 15 to 20 minutes | Makes: About 11 cups Muddy Buddies

9 cups Rice Chex or Corn Chex cereal

1 cup semisweet chocolate chips

½ cup creamy peanut butter

¼ cup butter

1 teaspoon vanilla extract

1½ cups powdered sugar

Pour cereal into large bowl and set aside.

In a 1-quart, microwave-safe bowl combine chocolate chips, peanut butter, and butter. Microwave on high power 1 to 1½ minutes, or until smooth, stirring after 1 minute.

Stir in vanilla and then pour chocolate sauce slowly over cereal. Gently stir mixture until cereal pieces are evenly coated.

Transfer cereal to a large, resealable plastic bag. Add powdered sugar, seal bag, and shake to coat well.

Spread on waxed paper to cool.

desserts

SNICKERS CHEESEBALL

Prep time: 15 minutes | Chilling time: 4 hours | Total time: 4 hours 15 minutes | Serves: 10

2 (8-ounce) bricks cream cheese, softened

¾ cup powdered sugar

2 tablespoons packed brown sugar

¾ cup creamy peanut butter

1 (7-ounce) jar marshmallow creme

22 Snickers Fun Size Snack Bars

In a large mixing bowl, cream together cream cheese, powdered sugar, brown sugar, peanut butter, and marshmallow creme with an electric mixer set to medium speed.

Unwrap and chop 7 of the Snickers Fun Size Snack Bars into sixths and fold them into the cream-cheese mixture.

Dump mixture in a pile onto a large piece of plastic wrap. Wrap well, forming the mixture into a ball as you go. Wrap ball in the other direction using a second piece of plastic wrap. Chill in refrigerator at least 4 hours to set.

After 4 hours, unwrap and coarsely chop remaining Snickers Fun Size Snack Bars.

Remove cheeseball from fridge, unwrap, reshape as necessary, and place on a serving plate. Press chopped Snickers into the cheeseball to cover completely. Cover loosely with plastic wrap and refrigerate until ready to serve.

Serve with vanilla wafers, graham cracker sticks, pretzels, or even apples.

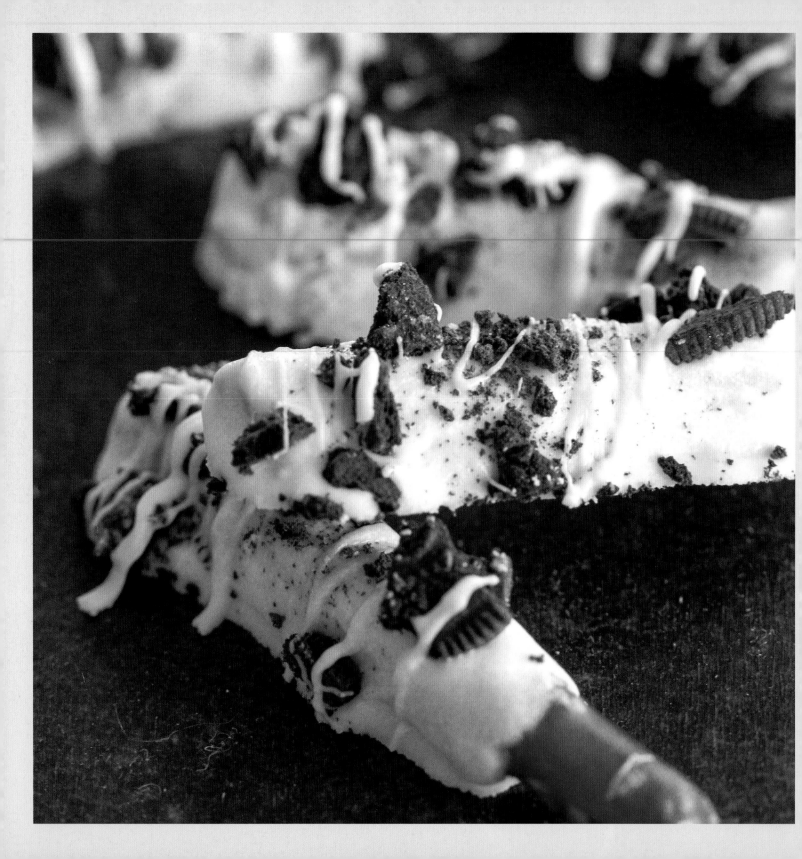

COOKIES-AND-CREAM CARAMEL PRETZEL RODS

Prep time: 25 minutes | Cooling time: 15 minutes | Total time: 35 minutes | Makes: 12 pretzel rods

12 large pretzel rods

1 cup unwrapped and melted caramel candies

1 cup white chocolate chips, melted

6 Oreo Cookies, crushed

Line a baking sheet with parchment paper and spray lightly with nonstick cooking spray.

Dip each pretzel rod in the caramel, making sure to cover pretzel rod halfway up. Place caramel-coated pretzel rod on greased parchment paper and let rest 5 to 10 minutes, until caramel sets and is completely cool. Repeat this process for remaining pretzel rods.

Once the caramel is set and cool, dip rods in melted white chocolate. Immediately sprinkle crushed Oreos over white chocolate, pressing crumbs into chocolate so they stick. Return rods to parchment paper and let set completely before serving.

CHOCOLATE-CARAMEL BROWNIE TRIFLE

Prep time: 20 minutes | Chilling time: 1 hour | Total time: 1 hour 20 minutes | Serves: 10

2 (3-ounce) boxes instant chocolate pudding mix

4 cups very cold milk

9 to 10 baked and cooled brownies (homemade or prepared from a mix), cut into 1-inch squares

1 (12-ounce) jar caramel sauce

4 (1.4-ounce) Heath or Skor candy bars, crushed

1 (16-ounce) tub frozen nondairy whipped topping, thawed, or 6 cups sweetened, freshly whipped cream

In a large bowl, prepare chocolate pudding by beating pudding mix into milk with a wire whisk. Beat for 2 minutes.

Spoon ⅓ of the pudding into the bottom of a trifle dish or large, clear glass bowl. Layer ⅓ of the brownie pieces on top of that, followed by just under a ⅓ of the crushed candy bars (you should have some left at the end to garnish the trifle with). Drizzle a few tablespoons caramel sauce evenly over that, and then top with ⅓ of the nondairy whipped topping or whipped cream. Repeat layers 2 more times, finishing with the nondairy whipped topping or whipped cream. Sprinkle remaining crushed candy bars on top to garnish.

Cover with plastic wrap and chill one hour before serving. This should be made the same day as it is served.

ONE-PAN TRIPLE-BERRY COBBLER

Prep time: 5 minutes | Cook time: 45 minutes | Total time: 50 minutes | Serves: 12

1 (36-ounce) bag frozen mixed berries

1 (15.25-ounce) yellow cake mix

½ cup (1 stick) butter, cut into small pieces

Preheat oven to 375 degrees F.

Dump frozen berries into 9x13-inch pan. Sprinkle the dry cake mix onto the frozen berries. Press the cake mix firmly into the berries, making sure they are all covered, but do not stir.

Cut ½ cup of butter into small slices. Layer them on top of the cake mix.

Bake for 45 minutes or until cake mix turns golden brown.

Serve warm, or with a scoop of vanilla ice cream on top.

BITE-SIZED CHERRY PIES

Prep time: 20 minutes | Cook time: 15 minutes | Total time: 35 minutes | Makes: 12 mini pies

1 (14.1-ounce) box Pillsbury refrigerated pie crusts, softened according to package directions

1 (20-ounce) can cherry pie filling

1 egg white

1 teaspoon vanilla

1 tablespoon milk

3 teaspoons granulated sugar

Preheat oven to 350 degrees F.

On a lightly floured surface, roll out each pie crust and cut into approximately 24 (2x3-inch) rectangles. Reshape and roll out any uneven pieces as needed to make each rectangle uniform in size.

Place a pie-crust rectangle on an ungreased baking sheet and spoon some pie filling (to include 3 or 4 cherries) onto the middle of it. Cover cherries with another pie-crust rectangle and use the tines of a fork to seal the edges all the way around. With a sharp paring knife, cut an X or V in the middle of each mini pie to allow the pie to vent any steam that builds up while baking. Repeat with remaining crusts and filling.

In a small bowl, whisk together egg white, vanilla, and milk until frothy. Brush egg wash over each mini pie and then sprinkle the tops with sugar.

Bake 12 to 15 minutes or until pie crust is cooked and golden brown in color.

CHERRY TURNOVERS

Prep time: 10 minutes | Cook time: 20 minutes | Total time: 30 minutes | Makes: 8 turnovers

1 (17.3-ounce) package frozen puff pastry sheets, thawed according to package directions

1 (21-ounce) can cherry pie filling

1 large egg, beaten

1½ cups powdered sugar

2 tablespoons milk

1 teaspoon vanilla extract

Preheat oven to 375 degrees F. Coat a rimmed baking sheet with nonstick cooking spray or line with parchment paper.

Unwrap puff pastry sheets and cut each sheet into 4 squares. Arrange squares on prepared baking sheet. Spoon 2 tablespoons cherry pie filling in the middle of each square. Brush the edges of each square with egg wash and fold squares in half to create a triangle. Use the tines of a fork to press and seal the edges of each turnover together. Brush extra egg wash on top of turnovers.

Bake 20 to 25 minutes, or until golden brown. Let cool slightly.

While turnovers cool, whisk together powdered sugar, milk, and vanilla in a small bowl to create a glaze. Drizzle glaze over warm turnovers and serve.